BIBLE STORY PICTURE CARDS

Toddlers & Twos

GROW

PROCLAIM · SERVE!

Grow your faith by leaps and bounds

GROW
PROCLAIM · SERVE!

Vol. 2 · No. 2   Winter 2013–14

EDITORIAL/DESIGN TEAM
Kerry Blackwood, Editor
Heidi Hewitt, Production Editor
Keitha Vincent, Designer
Anita Edlund, Writer

ADMINISTRATIVE TEAM
Neil M. Alexander, Publisher
**Marjorie M. Pon, Associate Publisher and
Editor of Church School Publications**
**Phillip D. Francis, Senior Design Manager,
Church School Publications**
LeeDell B. Stickler, Senior Editor, Children's Resources

Logo design: Marc Whitaker, MTWdesign
Background and frog: Shutterstock, Julien Tromeur
Cover design: Mark Foltz and Phillip D. Francis

GROW, PROCLAIM, SERVE: GROW YOUR FAITH BY LEAPS AND BOUNDS, TODDLERS AND TWOS, BIBLE STORY PICTURE CARDS: An official resource for The United Methodist Church approved by the General Board of Discipleship and published quarterly by Abingdon Press, a division of The United Methodist Publishing House, 201 Eighth Avenue, South, P.O. Box 801, Nashville, TN 37202-0801. Price: $4.99. Copyright © 2013 Abingdon Press. All rights reserved. Send address changes to GROW, PROCLAIM, SERVE: TODDLERS AND TWOS, BIBLE STORY PICTURE CARDS, Subscription Services, 201 Eighth Avenue, South, P.O. Box 801, Nashville, TN 37202-0801 or call 800-672-1789. Printed in the United States of America.

To order copies of this publication, call toll free: **800-672-1789**. You may fax your order to 800-445-8189. Telecommunication Device for the Deaf/Telex Telephone: 800-227-4091. Or order online at **cokesbury.com**. Use your Cokesbury account, American Express, Visa, Discover, or MasterCard.

If you have questions or comments, call Curric-U-Phone toll free: **800-251-8591**. Or e-mail **curricuphone@cokesbury.com**.

For information concerning permission to reproduce any material in this publication, write to Rights and Permissions, The United Methodist Publishing House, 201 Eighth Avenue, South, P.O. Box 801, Nashville, TN 37202-0801. You may fax your request to 615-749-6128, or e-mail *permissions@umpublishing.org*.

13 14 15 16 17 18 19 20 21 22—10 9 8 7 6 5 4 3 2 1

PACP01265060-01

Child Information Card

Today's date: _____

Full name of child: _____

Name child is called: _____

Date of birth: _____ Male _____ Female _____

Parents or guardians: _____

Phone numbers: _____

Address: _____

_____

E-mail: _____

People who live in the home with the child (name, relationship to child, age of other children in the home):

_____

_____

Allergies the child has, including food allergies: _____
_____

Is the child on any kind of regular medication? Yes _____ **No** _____
If yes, describe:

_____
_____

Is the child toilet trained? Yes _____ **No** _____

What are the words your child uses for toileting?

_____

Describe some of the activities your child enjoys: _____
_____

What words would you use to describe your child? _____
_____

Does your child attend daycare or preschool? Yes _____ **No** __

If yes, where? _____
_____

Please list anything else your child's teachers need to know to best m
child: _____

She gave birth to her firstborn child.
Luke 2:7, CEB

December I

Good News!

Sharing Faith With Your Child

Read this Bible story to your child.

The emperor made an important announcement. The emperor said that everyone had to go to their hometown and be counted. Mary and Joseph had to go to Bethlehem.

Mary was going to have a baby soon. Mary and Joseph's donkey went with them so that Mary could ride on it. When Mary and Joseph got to Bethlehem, the town was very busy. Many people were in Bethlehem to be counted.

There was no place for Mary and Joseph to sleep. Mary and Joseph looked and looked. Every place Mary and Joseph looked, people said, "Sorry, there is no room." Finally, a man said, "I don't have a room or a bed, but I have a stable where my animals stay." So, Mary and Joseph stayed in the stable with the animals.

That very night, Mary had her baby. The baby was a little boy, and Mary and Joseph named him Jesus. Mary wrapped Jesus in a blanket and placed him in the manger, where the animals ate their food.

There were some shepherds out in the field watching their sheep that night. An angel came to the shepherds and said, "Don't be afraid! I have some good news! A very special baby was born tonight in Bethlehem. You will find him wrapped in a blanket and lying in a manger."

As soon as the angel left, the shepherds said, "Let's go to Bethlehem! Let's go find this special baby." The shepherds found the baby, wrapped in a blanket and lying in a manger, just like the angel had said. It was baby Jesus.

Turn this card over and talk about the people in the picture. Help your child find Mary, Joseph, baby Jesus, and the donkey. Ask what other animals your child sees.

SAY: Mary had a very special baby. Mary's baby's name was Jesus.

GROW · **Proclaim** · **Serve** · Toddlers & Twos Bible Story Picture Cards
© 2013 Abingdon Press. Art: Mernie Gallagher-Cole/Portfolio Solutions

She gave birth to her firstborn child.
Luke 2:7, CEB

7

December 8

Good News!

Read this Bible story rhyme to your child.

Mary and Joseph went on a long trip
along with their donkey. Clip, clop, clop, clip.

They were so tired. They wanted to rest,
but the innkeeper said, "I have no rooms left."

Noooooo room! Noooooo room!

So Mary and Joseph did travel some more.
They came to an inn and knocked on the door.

Noooooo room! Noooooo room!

A little while later, one innkeeper said,
"I have a stable, but I have no bed."

So Mary and Joseph in the stable did stay.
The animals shared their manger and hay.

That special night, Mary's new baby came.
He was God's Son, and Jesus was his name!

The angel told the shepherds, "A baby is born
in Bethlehem, wrapped in a blanket so warm."

The shepherds went to find this special baby boy.
They found him like the angel said. Oh, what joy!

*Look at the picture of the angel and the shepherds on the front of
this card. Ask your child what the angel said to the shepherds.*

*Find the sheep and count them. Have your child glue a cotton ball
on each sheep.*

**SAY: When Jesus was born, Mary was happy, Joseph was
happy, the shepherds were happy, and the angel was happy.
Oh, what joy!**

GROW · **Proclaim** · **Serve** · Toddlers & Twos Bible Story Picture Cards
© 2013 Abingdon Press. Art: Mernie Gallagher-Cole/Portfolio Solutions

She gave birth to her firstborn child. Luke 2:7, CEB

December 15

Good News!

Sharing Faith With Your Child

Read this Bible story to your child.

The emperor made an important announcement. The emperor said that everyone had to go to their hometown and be counted. Mary and Joseph had to go to Bethlehem.

Mary was going to have a baby soon. Mary and Joseph's donkey went with them so that Mary could ride on it. When Mary and Joseph got to Bethlehem, the town was very busy. Many people were in Bethlehem to be counted.

There was no place for Mary and Joseph to sleep. Mary and Joseph looked and looked. Every place Mary and Joseph looked, people said, "Sorry, there is no room." Finally, a man said, "I don't have a room or a bed, but I have a stable where my animals stay." So, Mary and Joseph stayed in the stable with the animals.

That very night, Mary had her baby. The baby was a little boy, and Mary and Joseph named him Jesus. Mary wrapped Jesus in a blanket and placed him in the manger, where the animals ate their food.

There were some shepherds out in the field watching their sheep that night. An angel came to the shepherds and said, "Don't be afraid! I have some good news! A very special baby was born tonight in Bethlehem. You will find him wrapped in a blanket and lying in a manger."

As soon as the angel left, the shepherds said, "Let's go to Bethlehem! Let's go find this special baby." The shepherds found the baby, wrapped in a blanket and lying in a manger, just like the angel had said. It was baby Jesus.

Encourage your child to color the ornaments on the other side of this card. Cut the ornaments out, add a loop of yarn or a hook to each, and let your child name what is in each picture as he or she hangs the ornaments on your Christmas tree at home.

SAY: It's Christmas time. We celebrate the birthday of baby Jesus at Christmas time!

GROW • **Proclaim** • **Serve** • Toddlers & Twos Bible Story Picture Cards
© 2013 Abingdon Press. Art: Mernie Gallagher-Cole/Portfolio Solutions

Mary rocked him.
Mary rocked him.
Mary rocked her little babe.
Mary rocked him, for she loved him.
Mary rocked her little babe.

She gave birth to her firstborn child.
Luke 2:7, CEB

December 22

Good News!

Sharing Faith With Your Child

Sing the words below to the tune of "Oh My Darling, Clementine."
Show your child the motions for each verse.

(As you sing, march and shake your head "no.")
SING: There was no ro-om.
There was no ro-om.
There was no ro-om in the inn.
There was no room for baby Jesus.
There was no ro-om in the inn.

(As you sing, march and form a "roof" over your head—the tips of your fingers touching over your head.)
SING: In the stable,
in the stable,
that's where Jesus wa-as born.
In the stable, in the stable,
that's where Jesus wa-as born.

(Turn this card over and show your child the picture of baby Jesus. Then march and pretend to rock a baby in your arms as you sing.)
SING: Mary rocked him.
Mary rocked him.
Mary rocked her little babe.
Mary rocked him, for she loved him.
Mary rocked her little babe.

SAY: There were no rooms left in Bethlehem by the time Mary and Joseph got there. They stayed in a stable with the animals. The animals' food was put in a box called a manger. Mary wrapped her baby in a blanket and used the manger filled with hay for a bed for her new baby boy. Mary rocked her baby to sleep.

GROW · **Proclaim** · Serve · Toddlers & Twos Bible Story Picture Cards
© 2013 Abingdon Press. Art: Mernie Gallagher-Cole/Portfolio Solutions

She gave birth to her firstborn child.
Luke 2:7, CEB

13

December 29

Good News!

Sharing Faith With Your Child

Show your child the picture on the other side of this card. Ask if he or she can identify Mary, baby Jesus, Joseph, the shepherds, and the angel.

Read this Bible story of good news to your child.

SAY: A very special baby was born. His name was Jesus!
Mary was happy that Jesus was born.
Joseph was happy that Jesus was born.
The angel was happy that Jesus was born.
The shepherds were happy that Jesus was born.
I am happy that Jesus was born, too.
A very special baby was born. His name was Jesus!

Put a happy face sticker on each of your child's five fingers as you read the story again (one for Mary, one for Joseph, one for the angel, one for the shepherds, and one for "I.") If you do not have stickers, you can cut five circles from colored paper, draw a happy face on each circle, and put a loop of tape on the back of each one.

ASK: The angel had some happy news to tell. What did the angel say?

SAY: I have good news! A special baby is born in Bethlehem.

Sing this song to the tune of "Rock-a-Bye Baby." Invite your child to rock a doll in her or his arms while you sing the song together.

SING: Sleep, baby Jesus,
sleep on the hay.
Mary is singing.
Little lambs play.
Joseph is watching
stars shine so bright.
So sleep, baby Jesus,
sleep through the night.
Based on Luke 2:1-7
Words: Daphna Flegal and Linda Ray Miller

SAY: We are happy, too, that Jesus was born!

Jesus matured in wisdom and years. Luke 2:52, CEB

15

January 5
The Wise Men

Sharing Faith With Your Child

Read this Bible story to your child.

Long ago, there were some wise men watching the stars. One night, the wise men saw a very bright star. The star was so bright that the wise men decided to follow the star.

The wise men traveled for a long time. The wise men's camels went, too. The wise men stopped and asked the king, "Do you know where the special baby was born?"

The king said, "No, but go to Bethlehem and look for the baby. When you find the special baby, come back and tell me where the baby is."

The wise men saw the star again. This time, the wise men followed the star until the star stopped. That is when the wise men found the special baby, Jesus! But Jesus was not a baby anymore. Jesus was a little boy! Jesus was growing up.

How happy the wise men were! The wise men bowed down and worshipped Jesus. The wise men gave Jesus the gifts they had brought for him.

The wise men went to sleep that night and had a dream. In their dream, the wise men heard, "Do not go back to the king. The king will not worship Jesus." So the wise men went home a different way.

Have your child look at the picture on the front of this card. Invite your child to count the wise men in the big picture.

Show the child the three pictures on the side of the page. Encourage your child to find each wise man in the big picture.

SAY: The wise men saw a bright star in the sky. When the wise men followed the star, they found Jesus.

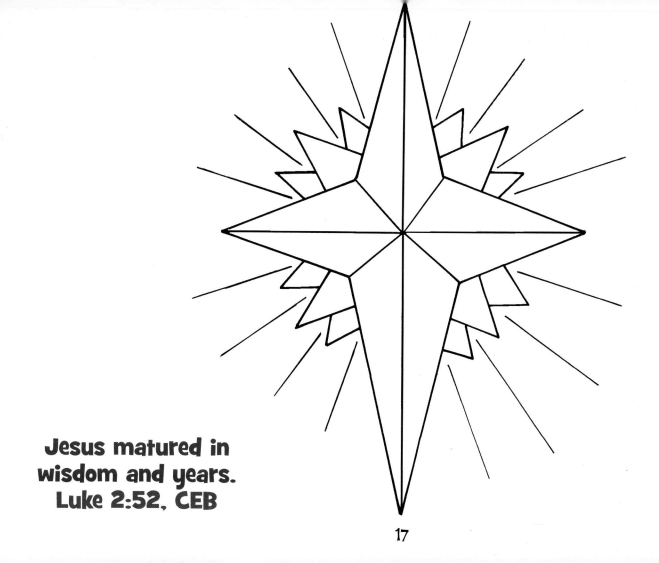

Jesus matured in wisdom and years.
Luke 2:52, CEB

January 12

The Wise Men

Sharing Faith With Your Child

Read this Bible story to your child.

It was dark outside. Wise men were watching the stars. One night, the wise men saw a very bright star. The star was so bright that the wise men decided to follow the star.

The wise men traveled for a long time. The wise men stopped and asked the king, "Do you know where the special baby was born?" The king said, "No, but go to Bethlehem and look for the baby. When you find the special baby, come back and tell me where the baby is."

The wise men saw the star again. This time, the wise men followed the star until the star stopped. That is when the wise men found the special baby, Jesus! But Jesus was not a baby anymore. Jesus was a little boy! Jesus was growing up.

How happy the wise men were! The wise men bowed down and worshipped Jesus. The wise men gave Jesus the gifts they had brought for him.

Invite your child to color the star with a bright color. Place the star on newspaper or in a shallow box lid. Add glue to the star, and help your child sprinkle glitter on top of the glue to make the star shine.

SAY: The wise men saw a bright star in the sky. The star was brighter than all the other stars. When the wise men followed the star, they found Jesus.

Jesus matured in wisdom and years.
Luke 2:52, CEB

January 19
The Wise Men

Sharing Faith With Your Child

Use the story rhyme and the motions with your child.

Star so light and star so bright,
  (Blink your fingers each time you say "star.")
the wise men followed you one night.
  (Point to the wise men in the picture on the other side of this card.)
Little Jesus they went to see.
  (Point to Jesus on this card.)
They took him gifts—1, 2, 3.
  (Point to the gifts in the wise men's hands on this card, and count them out loud.)

Star so light and star so bright,
  (Blink your fingers each time you say "star.")
let me tell you what I might.
  (Put your hands on either side of your mouth as if speaking.)
I love little Jesus, too.
  (Invite your child to point to Jesus on this card.)
In my heart and all the way through!
  (Point to your heart.)

Sing the following song with your child to the tune of "Twinkle, Twinkle, Little Star."

SING: Twinkle, twinkle, shining star,
guiding wise men from afar
to a home so far away,
where little Jesus played all day.
Twinkle, twinkle, shining star,
guiding wise men from afar.

Based on Matthew 2:1-12
Words: Sue Downing

SAY: When the wise men saw the bright star, they followed it. When the wise men found Jesus, he was not a baby anymore. Jesus was growing up, just like you are growing up.

GROW • **Proclaim** • **Serve** • Toddlers & Twos Bible Story Picture Cards
© 2013 Abingdon Press. Art: Deborah Borgo/Gwen Walters Artists' Rep.

Jesus matured in wisdom and years. Luke 2:52, CEB

January 26
The Wise Men

Sharing Faith With Your Child

Invite your child to count the wise men in the picture on the front of this card. Then have your child count the gifts. Encourage your child to use a crayon or a finger to trace the box around each gift.

Sing the words below to the tune of "The Wise Man Built His House Upon the Rock." (To hear the tune, go to kididdles.com and click on All Songs at the top of the page to search for the tune. It is under "Songs that start with W." After you click on the song title, click on the video of the song below the lyrics.)

SING: The wise men came to see the little child.
The wise men came to see the little child.
The wise men came to see the little child,
and they brought some gifts for him.

Another song that your child might enjoy learning and singing is "Jesus Grew" sung to the tune of "London Bridge Is Falling Down."

SING: Jesus grew just like we grow, *(Clap hands.)*
like we grow, like we grow.
Jesus grew just like we grow.
See me growing! *(Crouch down, then stretch up slowly to tiptoes with arms overhead.)*

We thank God for how we grow, *(Clap hands.)*
how we grow, how we grow.
We thank God for how we grow.
See me growing! *(Crouch down, then stretch up slowly to tiptoes with arms overhead.)*
Based on Luke 2:40

SAY: When the wise men saw Jesus, he wasn't a baby anymore. Jesus was about two years old. Jesus had grown up, just like you are growing up.

GROW · **Proclaim** · **Serve** · Toddlers & Twos Bible Story Picture Cards
© 2013 Abingdon Press. Art: Deborah Borgo/Gwen Walters Artists' Rep.

You could not work these miracles,
unless God were with you.
John 3:2, CEV

23

February 2
Jesus Calms the Storm

Sharing Faith With Your Child

Read this Bible story to your child.

Jesus and his friends were in a boat. Jesus was sound asleep. It began to rain. The wind began to blow. The waves rocked the boat. The rain came down harder. The wind blew harder. The waves rocked the boat harder, too.

The boat rocked so hard that the men were afraid. The men told Jesus, "Wake up!" Jesus knew that his friends were afraid. Jesus told the wind and the waves, "Be still!" Jesus' friends were surprised when the wind and the waves did what Jesus said.

Turn to the front of this card. Look at the faces along the side of the page. The men look scared. Jesus took care of them in the storm. Invite your child to find each face in the picture. Let your child make a scared face. Then invite your child to make a surprised face.

Teach your child this song to sing to the tune of "Row, Row, Row Your Boat."

SING: Row, row, row my boat
far out in the sea.
Merrily, merrily, merrily, merrily,
Jesus is with me.

SAY: Jesus is always with you. Jesus will help you feel better when you are afraid.

You could not work these miracles, unless God were with you.
John 3:2, CEV

25

February 9
Jesus Calms the Storm

Sharing Faith With Your Child

Read this shorter version of the Bible story to your child. Add the sound effects.

RAIN (**SAY:** Drip, drip.)
WIND (*Make a blowing sound.*)
THUNDER (*Clap loudly.*)
WAVES (**SAY:** Splash!)

SAY: There was RAIN, WIND, THUNDER.
The WAVES were big.
"Jesus, wake up!" the men shouted.
Jesus told the storm to be still.
No more RAIN.
No more WIND.
No more THUNDER.
No more WAVES.
Everything was quiet.
Jesus' friends were surprised to see what Jesus could do!

Have your child turn this card over to see the picture on the front. Remind your child that there was a big storm and that Jesus' friends were afraid. Invite your child to pose like Jesus in the picture and say, "Be still!" Then invite your child to say, "Jesus helps me!"

ASK: Who was in the boat with Jesus? (*Jesus' friends*)
What happened while Jesus and his friends were in the boat? (*A big storm came up.*)
What did Jesus tell the storm to do? (*Be still!*)
Did the storm stop? (*Yes.*)

SAY: Any time you are scared, ask Jesus to help you. Jesus will help you, just like Jesus helped his friends in the boat.

You could not work these miracles, unless God were with you.
John 3:2, CEV

27

February 16

Jesus Calms the Storm

Sharing Faith With Your Child

Look at the picture on the front of this card. Help your child notice the faces of Jesus' friends and of Jesus. Have your child circle each face that looks happy (all of them). Remind your child that it was raining very hard, but now the water was calm. Jesus calmed the storm!

Sing this Bible story with your child this week, using the tune of "The Wheels on the Bus." Add the motions.

SING: Jesus and his friends were in the boat, *(Rock gently from side to side.)*
in the boat, in the boat.
Jesus and his friends were in the boat,
in the boat.

The wind and the big waves tossed them 'round, *(Rock harder.)*
tossed them 'round, tossed them 'round.
The wind and the big waves tossed them 'round,
tossed them 'round.

(Whisper this verse.)
Jesus told the water, "Peace, be still!
Peace, be still! Peace, be still!"
Jesus told the water, "Peace, be still!
Peace, be still!"

The rain and the water settled down,
settled down, settled down.
The rain and the water settled down.
All were safe.

SAY: Jesus calmed the storm!

GROW · **Proclaim** · **Serve** · Toddlers & Twos Bible Story Picture Cards
© 2013 Abingdon Press. Art: Naoko Matsunaga/Gwen Walters Artists' Rep.

You could not work these miracles, unless God were with you.
John 3:2, CEV

29

February 23
Jesus Calms the Storm

Sharing Faith With Your Child

Read this Bible story to your child.

Jesus and his friends were in a boat. Jesus was sound asleep. It began to rain. The wind began to blow. The waves rocked the boat. The rain came down harder. The wind blew harder. The waves rocked the boat harder, too.

The boat rocked so hard that the men were afraid. The men told Jesus, "Wake up!" Jesus knew that his friends were afraid. Jesus told the wind and the waves, "Be still!" Jesus' friends were surprised when the wind and the waves did what Jesus said.

Talk about the picture the front of this card. Help your child count the fish in the water. Encourage your child to color the fish.

Read the story to your child again, but this time encourage your child to copy your motions while you tell the story.

Jesus and his friends were in a boat. (*Pretend to rock back and forth gently as if in a boat.*)
Jesus was sound asleep. (*Lay your head on you hands.*)

It began to rain. (*Ruffle your fingers downward to indicate rain.*)
The wind began to blow. (*Puff out your mouth as if blowing.*)
The waves rocked the boat. (*Pretend to rock the boat.*)
The rain came down harder. (*Rain harder with your fingers.*)
The wind blew harder. (*Blow harder with your mouth.*)
The waves rocked the boat harder, too. (*Pretend to rock the boat back and forth even harder.*)

The boat rocked so hard that the men were afraid. The men told Jesus, "Wake up!" (*Pretend to wake a sleeping person.*)
Jesus knew that his friends were afraid. Jesus told the wind and the waves, "Be still!" (*Put your arm out in a commanding way.*)
Jesus' friends were surprised when the wind and the waves did what Jesus said. (*Look surprised.*)

SAY: Jesus' friends were glad that Jesus told the storm to calm down. What an amazing thing Jesus did that day!

GROW · **Proclaim** · **Serve** · Toddlers & Twos Bible Story Picture Cards
© 2013 Abingdon Press. Art: Naoko Matsunaga/Gwen Walters Artists' Rep.

Celebrating Christmas With Your Toddler or Two-Year-Old

The Christmas season is upon us once again, and perhaps you want to help your child and family establish ways to celebrate this season by focusing on the true meaning of Christmas. But how do you do it? We live in a world that makes secular tradition almost impossible to ignore. Celebrating the birth of Christ can be done, though, and you can begin it this year with your small child. The celebrations and traditions you establish this year can change the way your family celebrates Christmas in the years ahead.

1. Use Nativity Sets. Nativity sets are a wonderful way to help your child learn the story of Jesus' birth. Obtain a wooden or plastic Nativity set, and keep it on a low table so your child can play with it. Name each person in the Nativity set and tell what his or her role was in the birth story. **SAY: This is Mary.** (*Hand Mary to your child.*) **Mary was Jesus' mother. Mary took care of Jesus and wrapped him snugly and laid him in a manger, because there was no room in Bethlehem.** (*Hand baby Jesus to your child.*) The way young children play with the people in the Nativity set is interesting. They often will do one of two things: line up the people in a straight line, or circle the people around baby Jesus. Either way, discuss the people, and let your child enjoy playing with them and retelling the Bible story.

2. Deliver Treats to Relatives, Neighbors, and Friends With a Scripture Passage Attached. Let your child help you make the treat, if at all possible. As soon as a child can stand safely on a chair, let him help make cookies. At first, all he can do is stir; but eventually he even will learn to crack eggs. My six-year-old granddaughter is better at shaping the cookie dough than I am. Let the child participate. It is not always easy and is often messy, but it means so much to both of you. Attach a Scripture verse to the treat, such as the following: "She gave birth to her firstborn child, a son, wrapped him snugly, and laid him in a manger, because there was no place for them in the guestroom" (Luke 2:7, CEB). "Your savior is born today in David's city. He is Christ the Lord" (Luke 2:11, CEB). "Glory to God in heaven, and on earth peace among those whom he favors" (Luke 2:14, CEB). Read the Scripture passages to your child. He or she will not be able to comprehend them completely, but most of us cannot completely comprehend God and God's miracles. It will help your child just to hear these familiar passages; and as she grows and develops in her faith, she will be able to understand the passages better. Then have your child help deliver the treats.

3. Use an Advent Calendar or an Advent Wreath. Children enjoy the fun of using an Advent calendar, which builds the anticipation until Christmas. There are many Advent calendars for sale, but buy the one that will help your child learn the birth story. Your family also can use Advent wreaths. They can be bought in Christian bookstores, or they can be made by using greenery, a Styrofoam circle, and candles. Most churches have family devotional books for families to use while lighting the Advent candles each Sunday before Christmas. While it will not

be safe to let your little child light the candles, he can watch and can blow out the candles. Again, though your child will not be able to understand the significance of Hope, Love, Joy, and Peace, he will be able to understand that getting ready to celebrate Jesus' birthday is very important.

4. Make a Birthday Cake for Baby Jesus. I started this tradition when my children were very young, and we still give Jesus a birthday cake for his birthday. We even sing the "Happy Birthday" song to Jesus. By doing this, you make Jesus very personal to your young child and help her understand that Jesus had a human side to him as well as a divine side. Young children will understand that Jesus is their friend.

Whatever this special Christmas season brings to you and your family, remember to hold your child more dearly each night, pray together, and thank God openly (in front of your child) for the gift of your child. Christmas reminds us that the very best things in life come in the form of a small child.

— *Kerry Blackwood*

Grow
PROCLAIM • SERVE!
GrowProclaimServe.com

ISBN-13: 978-1-426-76764-7

90000

9 781426 767647